Character Education

# Responsibility

by Lucia Raatma

**Consultant:**
Madonna Murphy, Ph.D.
Associate Professor of Education
University of St. Francis, Joliet, Illinois
Author, *Character Education in America's*
*Blue Ribbon Schools*

Bridgestone Books
an imprint of Capstone Press
Mankato, Minnesota

Bridgestone Books are published by Capstone Press,
151 Good Counsel Drive, P.O. Box 669, Mankato, Minnesota 56002.
www.capstonepress.com

Library of Congress Cataloging-in-Publication Data
Raatma, Lucia.
Responsibility/by Lucia Raatma.
p. cm.—(Character education)
Includes bibliographical references (p. 24) and index.
Summary: Explains the virtue of responsibility and how readers can practice it at home, in school, in the community, and with each other.
ISBN-13: 978-0-7368-0372-4 (hardcover)
ISBN-10: 0-7368-0372-6 (hardcover)
ISBN-13: 978-0-7368-9156-1 (softcover pbk.)
ISBN-10: 0-7368-9156-0 (softcover pbk.)
1. Responsibility—Juvenile literature. [1. Responsibility.] I. Title. II. Series.
BJ1451.R23  2000
179'.9—dc21
99-29182
CIP

**Editorial Credits**

Damian Koshnick and Christy Steele, editors; Heather Kindseth, cover designer and illustrator; Kimberly Danger, photo researcher

**Photo Credits**

David F. Clobes, 10, 14, 20
Index Stock Imagery, 18
Kent & Donna Dannen, 16
Photo Network/Myrleen Cates, 4; Paul Thompson, 8
Unicorn Stock Photos/Alice M. Prescott, 6; Joel Dexter, 12
Uniphoto/Ed Elberfeld, cover

072010
5843VMI

# Table of Contents

# Responsibility

Responsibility means doing what you say you will do. Responsible people try hard to keep their promises. They accept the consequences of their words or actions. Responsible people follow rules. People will trust you if you are responsible.

**consequence**

the result of an action

# Responsibility for Your Actions

Responsible people are honest. They do not blame others for their mistakes. They take responsibility for their actions. For example, your job may be to walk your family's dog. A responsible person would not play until the dog has been walked.

# Responsibility to Yourself

Being responsible to yourself means
trying your hardest. Always do your
best. Responsible people do not give up.
They practice batting if they strike out
in a game. Responsible people practice
a song until they can play it well.

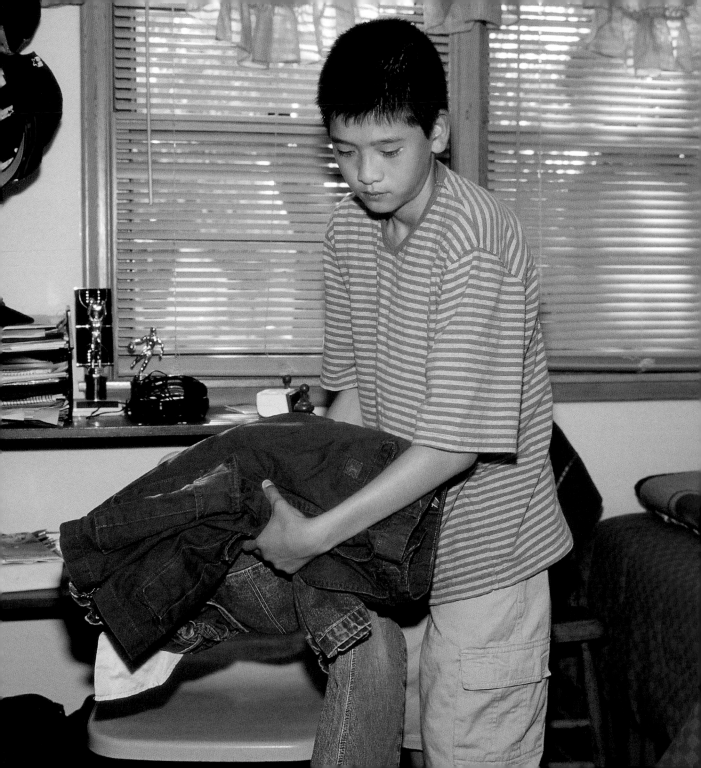

# Responsibility and Your Family

Being responsible means listening to your parents. It also means doing what they ask you to do. Your parents may ask you to keep your room clean. Cleaning your room shows your parents that you are responsible. Your parents will be proud when they see you acting responsibly.

## Responsibility with Your Friends

Responsible people do their best to be good friends. Being responsible means that you listen to your friends and keep their secrets. Responsible people also help their friends. You are responsible when you take care of your friends' belongings.

# Responsibility at School

Responsible students show respect for their teachers and classmates. You are responsible when you obey school rules. Responsible students are on time for school. They do their homework. Responsible people always try to do their best in school.

# The Environment

Everyone is responsible for taking care of the earth. You can be responsible for the environment in many ways. You can take pictures of wildflowers instead of picking them. You can shut off the water while you brush your teeth. This will save water. You also can recycle.

**environment**
the natural world around you

"Every man has a right to life. That means that he also has a right to make a comfortable living."
—Franklin D. Roosevelt

# Franklin D. Roosevelt

In 1932, Franklin D. Roosevelt became president of the United States. At that time, many people in the country had lost their jobs. Many people were poor. Franklin took responsibility for helping these people. He started programs that gave jobs to people.

# Responsibility and You

Responsibility is about trying to do the right thing. Responsible people try to keep their promises and follow the rules. Being responsible means doing your best. Responsible people are dependable. People will respect and trust you when you do what you promise.

**dependable**

able to be counted on

# ▼ Hands On: Plan a Party

Talk to your teacher about planning a class party. You could celebrate Valentine's Day, Thanksgiving, or other holidays.

**What You Need**

| | |
|---|---|
| paper plates | paper cups |
| soft drinks | food |
| games | decorations |
| tape | |

**What You Do**

1. Make a list of everything you need to prepare for the party.
2. Ask each student in your class to be responsible for one part of the party. For example, one person can make decorations.
3. Give a task to everyone in your class. Make sure that someone is responsible for the food, drinks, games, decorations, setting up, and cleaning up.
4. Have fun at the party.

# Words to Know

**consequence** (KON-suh-kwenss)—the result of an action

**dependable** (di-PEND-uh-buhl)—able to be counted on; people trust dependable people to do what they are supposed to do.

**environment** (en-VYE-ruhn-muhnt)—the natural world of the land, water, and air

**recycle** (ree-SYE-kuhl)—to make used items into new products; people can recycle items such as glass, plastic, newspapers, and aluminum cans.

## ▼ Read More

**Canning, Shelagh.** *Responsibility: Annie Shows Off.* Adventures from the Book of Virtues. New York: Aladdin Paperbacks, 1996.

**Pemberton, Nancy.** *The Child's World of Responsibility.* Chanhassen, Minn.: Child's World, 1998.

**Potts, Steve.** *Franklin D. Roosevelt: A Photo-Illustrated Biography.* Photo-Illustrated Biographies. Mankato, Minn.: Bridgestone Books, 1996.

## ▼ Internet Sites

FactHound offers a safe, fun way to find Internet sites related to this book.

Go to *www.facthound.com*

He'll fetch the best sites for you!

## ▼ Index